Stark County District Library
www.StarkLibrary.org
330.452.0665

MAY -- 2019

Y0-CJG-684

NATURAL MARVELS

Nature's Skyscrapers

WORLD BOOK

World Book, Inc.
180 North LaSalle Street, Suite 900
Chicago, Illinois 60601
USA

For information about other World Book publications, please visit our website at www.worldbook.com or call 1-800-WORLDBK (967-5325).

For information about sales to schools and libraries, please call 1-800-975-3250 (United States) or 1-800-837-5365 (Canada).

© 2017 World Book, Inc. All rights reserved. This volume may not be reproduced in whole or in part in any form without prior written permission from the publisher. WORLD BOOK and the GLOBE DEVICE are registered trademarks or trademarks of World Book, Inc.

Library of Congress Cataloging-in-Publication Data

Title: Nature's skyscrapers.
Description: Chicago: World Book, Inc., a Scott Fetzer Company, [2017] | Series: Natural marvels | Includes index.
Identifiers: LCCN 2016039106 | ISBN 9780716633686
Subjects: LCSH: Mountains--Juvenile literature. | Everest, Mount (China and Nepal)--Juvenile literature. | Teton Range (Wyo. and Idaho)--Juvenile literature. | Kilimanjaro, Mount (Tanzania)--Juvenile literature. | Chimborazo (Ecuador: Mountain)--Juvenile literature.
Classification: LCC GB512 .N38 2017 | DDC 551.43/2--dc23
LC record available at https://lccn.loc.gov/2016039106

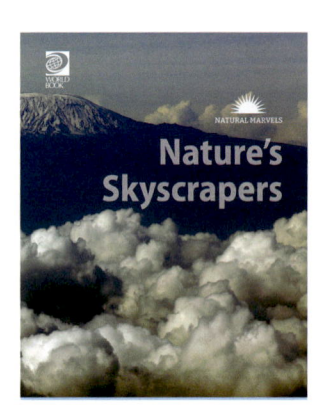

Over eons, the forces of nature have sculpted Earth in certain locations to create majestic landscapes of great beauty. Some of the most spectacular landforms are featured in this series of books. This image shows Kilimanjaro, Africa's highest mountain, from the air.

This edition:
ISBN: 978-0-7166-3368-6 (hc.)
ISBN: 978-0-7166-3363-1 (set, hc.)

Also available as:
ISBN: 978-0-7166-3377-8
(e-book, EPUB3)

Printed in China by Shenzhen Wing King Tong Paper Products Co., Ltd. Shenzhen, Guangdong
1st printing March 2017

STAFF

Writer: William D. Adams

Executive Committee

President
Jim O'Rourke

Vice President and Editor in Chief
Paul A. Kobasa

Vice President, Finance
Donald D. Keller

Vice President, Marketing
Jean Lin

Vice President, International Sales
Maksim Rutenberg

Director, Human Resources
Bev Ecker

Editorial

Director, Digital and Print Content Development
Emily Kline

Editor, Digital and Print Content Development
Kendra Muntz

Manager, Science
Jeff De La Rosa

Editors, Science
William D. Adams
Nicholas V. Kilzer

Administrative Assistant, Digital and Print Content Development
Ethel Matthews

Manager, Contracts & Compliance (Rights & Permissions)
Loranne K. Shields

Manager, Indexing Services
David Pofelski

Graphics and Design

Senior Art Director
Tom Evans

Senior Designer
Don Di Sante

Media Editor
Rosalia Bledsoe

Senior Cartographer
John M. Rejba

Manufacturing/Production

Production/Technology Manager
Anne Fritzinger

Proofreader
Nathalie Strassheim

Table of Contents

Introduction 4

Mount Everest 6

Where Is Mount Everest and
What's Special About it? 8

How Was Mount Everest Formed? 10

Who Explored Mount Everest? 12

The People of Mount Everest 14

Climbing Mount Everest Today 16

Teton Range 18

Where Is the Teton Range
and What's Special About It? 20

How Was the Teton Range Formed? 22

Kilimanjaro 24

Where Is Kilimanjaro and
What's Special About It? 26

How Was Kilimanjaro Formed? 28

About Kilimanjaro 30

Chimborazo 32

Where Is Chimborazo and
What's Special About It? 34

How Was Chimborazo Formed? 36

Glossary 38

Find Out More 39

Index 40

Glossary There is a glossary of terms on page 38. Terms defined in the glossary are in type **that looks like this** on their first appearance on any spread (two facing pages). Words that are difficult to say are followed by a pronunciation (*pruh NUHN see AY shuhn*) the first time they are used.

Introduction

Soaring high into the air, **mountains** are awe inspiring sights. People around the world have admired them throughout history, believing them to be places of great strength and power, and homes of spirits and gods. Today, some people take extreme risks and make huge efforts to climb mountains for the thrill of standing on top of the world.

In addition to people's appreciation of them, mountains form important natural boundaries. They serve as barriers between peoples, cultures, and countries. Mountains also break up *ecosystems* (communities of plants and animals), with different kinds of animals and plants living in the areas to either side. Some mountains reach so high that they affect the weather itself.

Scientists have learned much about mountains. They have learned that mountains can form in various ways, over extremely different time periods. Some mountains are young and still growing, for instance, and some are old and being worn down by **weathering** and **erosion** (ih ROH zhuhn). Explorers have mapped, climbed, and measured almost every mountain on Earth.

Read on to find out more about some of nature's skyscrapers. Learn where they are found, what makes them important to people, who discovered them, and who first climbed their heights. Then you can know what makes them some of nature's marvels.

A landform is a natural feature on Earth's surface, such as a mountain, river, or valley. This series of books, *Natural Marvels,* aims to show some of Earth's most amazing landforms and describe how they formed over time. Some landforms—certain volcanoes, for example—can form rather quickly. But, landforms are usually created over thousands or even millions of years. In these books, you will learn how forces on Earth can, over time, create landscapes of great beauty.

TETON RANGE

CHIMBORAZO

KILIMANJARO

MOUNT EVEREST

Mount Everest

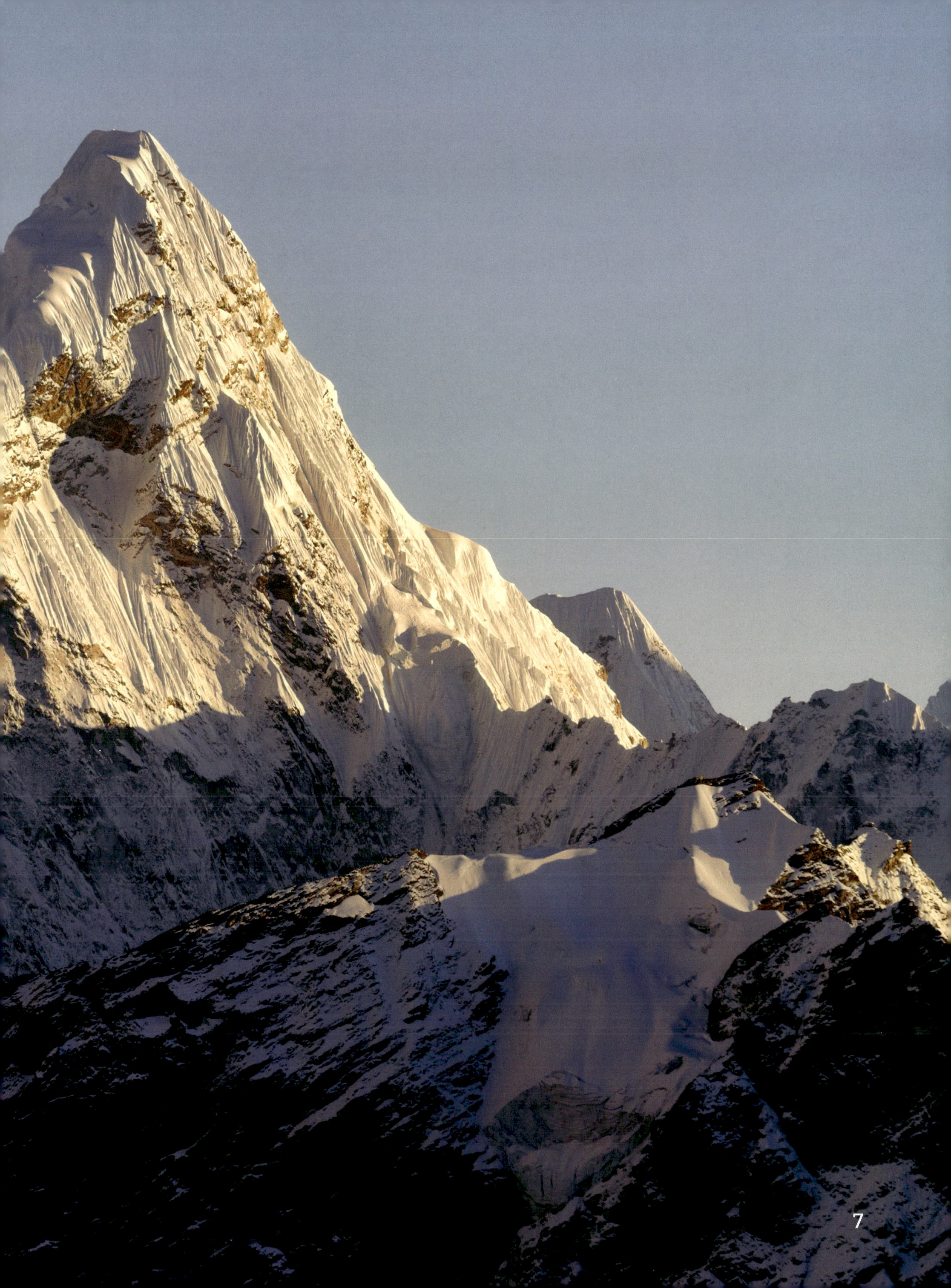

Where Is Mount Everest and What's Special About It?

At 29,035 feet (8,850 meters) above sea level, Mount Everest is the tallest **mountain** in the world. Part of the Himalaya mountain range, it is a giant among giants. Thirty-two of the tallest 50 mountains in the world are found in the Himalaya.

Mount Everest forms part of the border between Nepal and Tibet. Nepal is a tiny, mountainous country wedged between India and China. Tibet is a land in south-central Asia. It is often called the *Roof of the World* because it sits at such a high elevation. In addition to bordering the Himalaya and other large mountain ranges, most of the region sits on a high **plateau** (*pla TOH*).

The Himalaya form a huge wall between the **subcontinent** of India and the rest of Asia. Many rivers in the countries of India and Pakistan, such as the Ganges and Indus, start in the Himalaya, providing water for over a billion people. Along with the Plateau of Tibet, the mountain range blocks warm, moist air from the Indian Ocean from entering the rest of Asia, resulting in dry deserts there and the heavy rains of the monsoon season on the Indian subcontinent.

A view of Mount Everest, the tallest mountain in the world, as seen by climbers as they begin their ascent towards the summit.

WHY "EVEREST"?

When the British Surveyor General of India George Everest retired in 1843, his successor, A. S. Waugh, campaigned to name a peak after him. He chose a mountain that had been recently calculated to be the tallest in the Himalayan chain. The name was formally adopted in 1865. In doing this, Waugh ignored Great Britain's tradition of using local names for peaks—a tradition George Everest himself followed. Tibetans still call the mountain *Chomolungma* (goddess mother of mountains), however, and Nepalese call it *Sagarmatha* (head of the sky).

A stone monument called a stupa (above) marks a place for quiet meditation, reflection, and prayer near Mount Everest.

How Was Mount Everest Formed?

Mount Everest, like many landforms on Earth, formed as a result of **plate tectonics**. Plate tectonics describes Earth's surface as made up of about 30 rigid pieces called tectonic plates, or just plates. The plates make up **continents** and the ocean floor. Over the course of millions of years, plates pull apart and crash into each other, forming many of Earth's surface features.

Most of the changes to Earth's surface occur slowly and are not noticeable over a human lifetime. But earthquakes and the eruption of **volcanoes** are occasional violent reminders that Earth's surface is always changing around us.

The Himalaya are **fold-thrust mountains**. This kind of **mountain** forms when two tectonic plates collide head-on. Millions of years ago, Earth's continents were arranged much differently than they are today. About 100 million years ago, the plate that makes up the **subcontinent** of India split off from Africa and began drifting north towards the plate that makes up the continent of Asia. The land masses started colliding about 50 million years ago in a slow-motion crash. Over the next 50 million years, the plates' edges folded and crumpled as rock from Asia was thrust up over the rock layers of the Indian plate. The Himalaya formed from these uplifted rocks which are still being pushed upward today.

STILL GROWING

Every year, many mountaineers (above) try to reach the peak of Everest (left). Each year, every climber that reaches the top of Everest climbs a little bit higher than the last! That is because Everest, the tallest mountain in the world, is still growing taller. The two enormous tectonic plates that first collided head-on millions of years ago have not yet stopped moving. This continuing slow-motion crash pushes the entire Himalaya range upward at a rate of more than 0.5 inch (1 centimeter) per year.

11

Who Explored Mount Everest?

For hundreds of years, the area of Mount Everest was a blank space on Western maps. In the late 1700's, British explorers began to **survey** the region as part of their takeover of India. It eventually became clear that the Himalaya range was the tallest on Earth, and that Everest was the tallest peak of the range. Starting in the early 1900's, teams of mountaineers made several unsuccessful attempts to climb the peak. They had crude equipment and little understanding of the **mountain.** Though many teams climbed higher than anyone had gone before, none was able to reach the top.

In 1924, British mountaineer George Mallory and his climbing partner Andrew Irvine left a high camp in a trek towards the summit, never to return. In 1999, climbers found Mallory's frozen body on the slopes. Historians and mountaineers still debate whether Mallory and Irvine reached the summit before losing their lives.

Everest continued to resist attempts to climb it until 1953. That year, the British government led a massive operation to conquer the mountain. The operation involved dozens of support staff and created many well-stocked camps along the way. During this expedition, Edmund Hillary of New Zealand and Sherpa Tenzing Norgay became the first two people known to reach the top of Mount Everest and return.

Today, many Sherpa, the native people of Nepal, work as guides for mountaineering expeditions in the Himalaya range (left). Edmund Hillary (below left) of New Zealand and Sherpa guide Tenzing Norgay (below right) became the first two people to reach the top of Mount Everest and return. They reached the summit on May 29, 1953, and remained there for about 15 minutes before starting their descent.

The People of Mount Everest

The Sherpas are an ethnic group who live high in the Himalaya. The Sherpas probably moved to Nepal in the early 1500's from eastern Tibet. They still follow many of the customs and traditions of their Tibetan ancestors. Most of them practice the Tibetan Buddhist religion and regard the **mountain** as sacred. Out of reverence, they did not climb Mount Everest before contact with Europeans. Impressed by their climbing skills and resistance to **altitude sickness,** early European expeditions offered Sherpa men jobs carrying equipment, preparing climbing paths, and setting up camps. In 1953, Sherpa guide Tenzing Norgay became one of the first two people to ascend Mount Everest.

Today Sherpa men are as important as ever to Everest expeditions. They are drawn to jobs as mountain guides and porters by high salaries compared to those in the rest of the country. They still prepare paths up the mountain and haul gear for climbers, as they have for nearly a century.

Due to the difficulty of such work at extreme altitudes, many climbing Sherpas die on the job. After a deadly **avalanche** in 2014 in which 16 Sherpas were killed, many questioned whether it was worth continuing to risk their lives to work on the mountain. With huge demand for Everest expeditions and few other career prospects, however, most returned to work in 2015. That year, avalanches killed ten more Sherpas.

Sherpa guides readying their loads for a mountaineering expedition in the Himalaya range.

SACRED CEREMONY

Sherpas practice a form of Buddhism called *Lamaism*, a traditional religion of Tibet that regards Mount Everest as a sacred place. Most Sherpas attend a ceremony called a *puja* before they begin a climb. In this ceremony, Buddhist religious leaders, called *Lamas*, provide offerings to the gods of the mountain and bless the people and equipment on the expedition. Sherpas often invite Western climbers to the pujas, allowing them to join the blessing and experience an aspect of Sherpa culture. The ceremony also strengthens bonds of friendship between the guides and climbers.

A Sherpa man (above) paints a Buddhist prayer on a large stone on the route to Mt. Everest frequented by climbers.

15

Climbing Mount Everest Today

Climbing Mount Everest is considered one of the greatest mountaineering achievements on Earth. Since Hillary and Norgay first conquered it in 1953, thousands of people have flocked to the **mountain** to attempt the feat. Many have succeeded, but thousands have been forced to turn back due to poor weather conditions, **altitude sickness,** or injury. Hundreds more have died. Still, mountaineers come each year, lured by the magic of the world's tallest peak.

Everest presents many challenges to even the most skilled climbers. They must cross the Khumbu Icefall, a dangerous spot where shifting ice can crush climbers or cast them into deep *chasms* (deep narrow valleys). The last part of the climb lies above 26,000 feet (8,000 meters), known as the *death zone*, where the levels of oxygen in the air are so low that climbers may slowly suffocate. Most use bottled oxygen to survive. Even so, they are limited to spending only a few days at this level due to the effects of exhaustion and lack of oxygen.

Climbing Everest is extremely dangerous. Injury and death can come in many forms, from falls to freezing cold. The year 1996 was especially dangerous because an unexpected storm killed eight climbers, and **avalanches** killed over 20. No one reached the summit of Everest that year for the first time in over 40 years. The deaths led some people to question whether officials should limit the number of people who try to climb Everest.

TRASH AT THE TOP

Hundreds of mountaineers attempt to reach the summit of Everest each year. As they climb Everest, they often discard items they no longer need, such as food wrappers, empty oxygen tanks, and even human waste. Dangerous weather conditions on the slopes make it nearly impossible to collect these discarded items. Over time, this trash has begun to pile up. Furthermore, since it is too hazardous to remove them, the frozen bodies of climbers killed in accidents are often left where they fell. The bodies serve as grim landmarks on the dangerous trek up the mountain. In recent years, government officials and mountaineering organizations have increased efforts to remove trash from the slopes of Everest. Others have attempted to retrieve the dead bodies of fallen climbers.

Teton Range

19

Where Is the Teton Range and What's Special About It?

The jagged peaks of the Teton Range soar above the landscape of the state of Wyoming in the western United States. Not far from the famous Yellowstone National Park, the **mountains** are a site of stunning natural beauty. The highest peak is Grand Teton, which rises 13,770 feet (4,197 meters) above sea level. Overall, the range is 40 miles (64 kilometers) long and 10 to 15 miles (16 to 24 kilometers) wide.

For thousands of years, Native Americans came to a valley near the Tetons (now called Jackson Hole) in the summer months to take advantage of the region's natural resources. Starting around 1800, American and European fur trappers hunted for beavers and other small **mammals**. Since about 1900, people have come just to enjoy its scenic beauty. People there built *dude ranches,* quaint resorts where visitors experienced a cleaned-up version of western pioneer life. Grand Teton National Park was created by the U.S. government in 1950 to protect the range, which remains a popular tourist destination.

The Tetons are home to many animals, including bald eagles, bears, elk, bighorn sheep, bison, sandhill cranes, and trumpeter swans. Although the summers are warm and lush, the winters are cold and unforgiving. Animals cope with the cold winters in different ways. Some, such as birds and pronghorn antelope, leave the area during the winter. Others, such as bears and ground squirrels, stay and **hibernate** through the winter.

A pair of elk (left) graze leisurely during the harsh Wyoming winter at the National Elk Refuge in Jackson Hole, at the foot of the Teton Range.

21

How Was the Teton Range Formed?

The Tetons are **fault-block mountains,** formed where the North American **tectonic plate** is pulling apart or **rifting.** The stretching of Earth's **crust** produces fractures called **faults.** Huge blocks of crust tilt or push up along these faults, while neighboring regions drop down to form **basins.** The land to the west of the fault pushed up to form the Teton Range, while the east dropped down and became Jackson Hole.

The Tetons are some of the youngest **mountains** in North America. They began forming about 10 million years ago. By this time, the continents had moved near their present locations. Because they are so young, the Tetons lack *foothills*. These are smaller mountains at the base of larger ones that are created by **erosion.** Since erosion has not had enough time to form foothills, the Tetons rise dramatically up from the valley floor. Although the mountains themselves are young, the rocks they are made of are some of the oldest on Earth. The core rocks of the Tetons were formed some 3 billion years ago.

The Shoshone people, who have lived in this region for thousands of years, use the word *teewinot* to describe the many peaks of the Teton Range. The name Teton comes from early French-speaking explorers of the area.

WHO WAS FIRST?

Historians do not know for sure who first climbed Grand Teton. In 1872, Nathaniel P. Langford and James Stevenson claimed to have reached the top. However, surveyor William Owen disputed the claim. Owen wrote that there was no evidence of the 1872 expedition when he reached the summit with his team (above) in August 1898. He wrote that Langford and Stevenson's descriptions of the peak did not match what he saw there.

Mount Moran (left) rises steeply from the surrounding valley in the Teton Range. The mountains in this region lack small foothills at their base because they were formed relatively recently in Earth's history.

Kilimanjaro

25

Where Is Kilimanjaro and What's Special About It?

Africa's highest **mountain** is found in the northern part of the country of Tanzania, near the border with Kenya in East Africa. Kilimanjaro towers over the **savanna,** its snowcapped peak providing a breathtaking backdrop to the surrounding wildlife parks. Kilimanjaro's highest point, Uhuru Peak, is 19,340 feet (5,895 meters) above sea level. The fertile soils and meltwater from its **glaciers** make the surrounding area valuable farmland. It is also a popular tourist destination. Some 35,000 people visit Kilimanjaro each year to climb the peak or enjoy viewing the wildlife that lives around its base.

In 1848, German missionaries Johannes Rebmann and Johannes Krapf became the first Europeans to see the mountain. They were surprised to find a snow-covered mountain so close to the equator, and some mapmakers back in Europe refused to believe their account. But it is so cold at the heights of Kilimanjaro that they are home to year-round snow, and even glaciers. After a spirited race between European climbers, German Hans Meyer and Austrian Ludwig Purtscheller became the first people to reach the summit, in 1889.

Kilimanjaro's glaciers have been shrinking ever since they were first seen by Europeans. Hans Meyer himself, in a journey back to Kilimanjaro in 1898, was amazed at how far the glaciers had retreated. Many scientists predict that they will disappear completely by about the year 2030 due to the warming of Earth's surface caused by climate change.

The savanna surrounding Kilimanjaro is home to animals, such as elephants (below), that attract many tourists.

How Was Kilimanjaro Formed?

Unlike Mount Everest and the Tetons, which formed when **tectonic plates** collided or split, some **mountains** are produced by the eruption of molten rock that builds up as it cools. These are **volcanic mountains**. Tectonic forces are still responsible for the formation of volcanic mountains, however. It is the movement of the Earth's plates that causes heat and pressure to build up under the surfaces and form **volcanoes**.

Kilimanjaro is a **stratovolcano** composed of three different volcanic peaks. Eruptions began about 2.5 million years ago, at the Shira volcano. It collapsed around 1.9 million years ago and now forms a broad **plateau** west of the main peak. About 1 million years ago, the Mawenzi (also spelled Mawensi) and Kibo peaks began to form. No volcanic activity has been observed for hundreds of years, but the Kibo summit is considered **dormant**, rather than **extinct**, meaning it could erupt again at any time. At this peak, climbers often notice a sulfurous smell and that the ground is warm to the touch, signs that **magma** lies not far below.

Kilimanjaro is part of a long arc of volcanic mountains at the Great Rift Valley, a huge split in Earth's surface that cuts through eastern Africa. Forces within the Earth are pushing parts of Africa apart. At the site of this spreading, the Great Rift Valley has formed. Since Earth's **crust** here is not as thick as it is in other places, magma can rise to the surface and form volcanoes.

Uhuru Peak, seen here, on the Kibo summit is the highest point on Kilimanjaro at 19,340 feet (5,895 meters) above sea level.

LOCAL LEGENDS

Kilimanjaro's two tallest summits are named Kibo and Mawenzi. Kibo is the highest and Mawenzi is second. Local folklore explains why the two summits look so different. According to tradition, Kibo and Mawenzi were neighbors. One day, Mawenzi's fire went out, so he asked Kibo for some burning embers to restart it. Kibo happily gave him some embers from his own hearth. On his way home, Mawenzi decided to play a joke on Kibo. He threw the embers away and returned to Kibo to beg for more. Kibo grudgingly gave him more embers. Again Mawenzi threw them away and returned. Kibo, realizing he was being tricked, became angry and beat Mawenzi. This is why the Mawenzi peak is smaller and looks crushed and jagged compared to Kibo.

A sign post (above) on one of Kilimanjaro's trails directs climbers to Kibo and Mawenzi summits and to Horombo, a rest camp for climbers.

About Kilimanjaro

PROTECTED

Kilimanjaro National Park occupies an area of 186,201 acres (75,353 hectares) that includes both the **volcano** and the surrounding plains. Kilimanjaro is surrounded by **savanna** inhabited by a wide variety of wildlife, some of them endangered species.

Because of its height, there are different environments with their own characteristics at Kilimanjaro.

- Bare rock and ice
- Alpine environment
- Heath and shrub
- Cloud forest
- Rain forest
- Savanna and farmland

35,000
The estimated number of people visiting Kilimanjaro each year.

Shira cliff

Shira Cone
The oldest and most **eroded** of the three volcanic cones of Kilimanjaro. Its height is 13,000 feet (3,962 meters) above sea level.

Experts estimate that if the trend continues, by 2030 the great mountain will have completely lost its icecap.

RECEDING GLACIERS

The **glacier** of Kilimanjaro is one of the area's major environmental problems. It is shrinking due to warming of the climate.

1993

2000

The surrounding plains are home to many large mammals, including lions, zebras, and elephants (shown).

Mount Kilimanjaro is in Africa's Great Rift Valley
The **mountain** stands alone on the plain of Tanzania. But it is part of a series of volcanic mountains and craters in Africa's Great Rift Valley. This image shows how Kilimanjaro's three peaks line up with nearby volcanic mountains oriented from east to west.

Monduli · Meru · Nguurdoto crater · Shira · Kibo · Mawenzi

Kibo cone
The youngest of the cones, its profile is rounded with gentle slopes. This cone is **dormant** and could still erupt.

19,340 FEET (5,895 METERS)
Kilimanjaro rises above the surrounding plains. It is one of the highest volcanoes in the world.

Three in One
Kilimanjaro is actually made up of three volcanic cones: Kibo, Mawenzi, and Shira. Uhuru Peak on the Kibo cone is the highest point of Kilimanjaro.

Reusch crater

The Saddle
This broad valley, between Kibo and Mawenzi, is at 11,811 feet (3,600 meters) above sea level. It is a cold, dry, and treeless region.

Breach Wall
This wall borders a deep valley formed by an ancient landslide.

Uhuru Peak at Kibo
A sign in English welcomes climbers at the top of Kilimanjaro, 19,340 feet (5,895 meters).

Boundary of Kilimanjaro National Park

Mawenzi Cone
At 16,893 feet (5,149 meters), Mawenzi is Africa's third highest peak. Although the Kibo cone is on the same mountain, Mawenzi is quite different, with a steep profile.

Km
0   5

Chimborazo

33

Where Is Chimborazo and What's Special About It?

Chimborazo, at 20,702 feet (6,310 meters) above sea level, is the largest **mountain** in the South American country of Ecuador. For many years, people thought Chimborazo was the tallest mountain in the world. This was partly due to the fact that the remoteness of the Himalaya in Asia and many other peaks in the Andes made them hard to measure. Chimborazo is a lone peak, and is therefore much easier to measure from the surrounding plains. When they were measured accurately, it became clear that many other peaks are even taller than Chimborazo.

German explorer and naturalist Alexander von Humboldt attempted to climb Chimborazo in 1802, while on an expedition to Central and South America. He did not succeed, but he reached a higher point than any European had at the time. His account of the mountain fascinated people in Europe and inspired new attempts by others. English mountaineer Edward Whymper and Italian brothers Jean-Antoine and Louis Carrel finally reached the peak in 1880. Whymper climbed the mountain again later that year with a different party.

Sheep graze on the fertile slopes of the Andes Mountains around the snowcapped peak of Chimborazo in Ecuador.

EARTH'S HIGH POINT

Although Mount Everest is taller when considering height above sea level, the peak of Chimborazo is actually the farthest point of land from the center of Earth. Earth is not quite a perfect sphere. As it spins on its axis, the rotation causes Earth to bulge slightly near the middle. Despite being almost 2 miles (3 kilometers) shorter than Everest in terms of height above sea level, the peak of Chimborazo is about 1.5 miles (2.5 kilometers) farther from the center of Earth, since it is so much closer to the bulging equator than Everest.

Chimborazo is the highest of about 35 peaks in northern Ecuador that form an "avenue of volcanoes" (below).

How Was Chimborazo Formed?

Like Kilimanjaro, Chimborazo is a **volcanic mountain** and a **stratovolcano.** Unlike Kilimanjaro, however, which formed as the result of **tectonic plates** pulling apart, Chimborazo formed as a result of two plates colliding. This is similar to how Mount Everest was formed, but with one key difference: the collision was between a plate edge made of oceanic **crust** and one made of **continental** crust, rather than two plate edges of continental crust. Continental crust is less dense than oceanic crust, so when the two collide, the oceanic crust slides under the continental crust.

Deep under the Pacific Ocean near the west coast of South America, the Pacific plate is sliding under the South American plate. As it sinks down into Earth, some of the Pacific plate rocks melt. This resulting hot **magma** forces its way through the South American plate to the surface, forming Chimborazo along with a line of other **volcanoes.**

Chimborazo is one of the youngest mountains in the world. It began to form less than 100,000 years ago. The mountain has collapsed twice in its history, only to be built up again with further eruptions. Like Kilimanjaro, Chimborazo is now considered **dormant.** It last erupted some 1,500 years ago, but it could erupt again at any time.

RISING MAGMA

The Black Hills of South Dakota (above) in the United States also formed as a result of rising magma. However, the magma never reached Earth's surface. Instead, it pooled under the surface, pushing up a broad dome of crust. As the dome rose above its surroundings, it became subject to **erosion.** The softer outer layers of rock are worn away by wind and rain. The harder rock below eroded unevenly, forming sharp peaks and valleys.

Chimborazo (left) was formed by magma rising within Earth. But the magma was forced up to the surface, so this young mountain looks very different compared to the Black Hills.

Glossary

altitude sickness illness caused by lack of oxygen in the blood and body tissues at great height

avalanche a mass of snow that slides down a mountain slope

basin a low region drained by a river and the streams that flow into it

continent a part of Earth's surface that forms one of the great dry-land masses

crust the upper layer of Earth, made of solid rock

dormant describes an active volcano that is not currently erupting or showing signs of a coming eruption

erosion the gradual eating into or wearing away of Earth's surface by glaciers, temperature changes, running water, waves, ice, or wind

extinct describes a volcano that will probably never erupt again

fault a fracture or crack in Earth's crust

fault-block mountain mountain that forms where tectonic plates are pulling apart

fold-thrust mountain mountain that forms when two tectonic plates collide head-on

glacier a large mass of ice that flows slowly over Earth's surface under the influence of gravity

hibernation is an inactive, sleeplike state that some animals enter during the winter

magma molten rock below the ground

mammal warm-blooded animal that feeds its young on the mother's milk

mountain a landform that stands much higher than the surrounding terrain

plate tectonics describes that Earth has an outer shell made up of rigid pieces, called tectonic plates, that move over time. Plate tectonics explains the origin of most of the major features of Earth's surface

plateau a raised area of relatively flat land

rifting the separation or spreading of one or more plates

savanna also spelled savannah, a grassland with widely scattered trees and shrubs

stratovolcano cone-shaped volcano with steep sides

subcontinent a large land mass that is smaller than a continent

survey to measure size, shape, position, or boundaries of land

tectonic plate one of the rigid pieces of rock that make up Earth's outer surface

volcanic mountain mountain formed by the eruption of molten rock and its build-up as it cools

volcano a place where ash, gases, and molten rock from deep underground erupt onto Earth's surface

weathering the destructive action of air, water, or frost on rock

Find Out More

Mountains by Chris Oxlade (Raintree, 2015)
This book describes what climbers need to bring in order to explore a mountain.

Mountains Inside Out by James Bow (Crabtree Publishing Company, 2015)
Discover the organisms that live in a mountainous ecosystem.

Mountain: Portraits of High Places by Sandy Hill (Rizzoli, 2011) *A collection of gorgeous images collected by lifelong mountaineer Sandy Hill.*

Use Your Noodle!

Mountains can be barriers to travel, but they also provide many benefits to people. Think about the resources that come from mountains, from water to minerals. Consider the certain kinds of plants and animals that thrive on mountainous *habitats* (areas in which to live). What do you think life would be like if there were no mountains or mountain ranges?

Acknowledgments

Cover	© Joseph Sohm, Shutterstock
4-5	© Hitendra Sinkar, Alamy Images
6-7	© iStock
8-9	© Daniel Prudek, iStock; © Dmitry Reznichenko, Shutterstock
10-11	© Pichugin Dmitry, Shutterstock; © iStock
12-13	© Gordon Wiltsie, Getty Images; © Keystone Pictures USA/Alamy Images
14-15	© iStock; © Kevin Frayer, AP Photo
16-17	© Daniel Prudek, Shutterstock; © Binod Joshi, AP Photo
18-19	© Shutterstock
20-21	© Philip Mugridge, Alamy Images
22-23	© age footstock/Alamy Images; National Park Service
24-25	© Joseph Sohm, Shutterstock
26-27	© Graeme Shannon, Shutterstock
28-29	© Smolina Marianna, Shutterstock; © Shutterstock
30-31	© Sol 90 Images
32-33	© Dr Morley Read, Shutterstock
34-35	© Shutterstock; © Ksenia Ragozina, Shutterstock
36-37	© Steve Bloom Images/SuperStock; © age footstock/Alamy Images

Index

A
altitude sickness, 14, 16
Andes Mountains, 34
animals, 20-21, 26-27, 34-35
avalanches, 14, 16

B
basins, 22
Black Hills, 37
Buddhism, 14, 15

C
Carrel, Jean-Antoine and Louis, 34
Chimborazo, 32-37; features of, 35-36; formation of, 36-37; map, 5
climate change, 26
continental crust, 36
continents, 10
crust, 28, 36

D
death zone, 16
dormant volcanoes, 28, 36
dude ranches, 20

E
Earth, shape of, 35
ecosystems, 4
Ecuador, 34, 35
elephants, 27, 30
elk, 20-21
erosion, 4, 22, 37
Everest, George, 9

F
fault-block mountains, 22
faults, 22
fold-thrust mountains, 10
foothills, 22

G
glaciers, 26, 30
Grand Teton, 20
Great Rift Valley, 28, 31

H
Hillary, Edmund, 12-13, 16
Himalaya, 8, 12, 34; formation of, 10
Humboldt, Alexander von, 34

I
Indian subcontinent, 8, 10
Irvine, Andrew, 12

K
Khumbu Icefall, 16
Kibo Cone, 28, 29, 31
Kilimanjaro, 24-31, 36; features of, 26-27, 30-31; formation of, 28; legends about, 29; map, 5
Krapf, Johannes, 26

L
Lamaism, 15
landforms, 5
Langford, Nathaniel P., 23

M
magma, 28, 36, 37
Mallory, George, 12
Mawenzi Cone, 28, 29, 31
Meyer, Hans, 26
Mount Everest, 6-17, 35, 36; climbing today, 16-17; exploration of, 12-13; features of, 8; formation of, 10-11; map, 5; names for, 9; people of, 14-15
Mount Kilimanjaro. *See* Kilimanjaro
Mount Moran, 22-23
mountaineering, on Mount Everest, 11; early, 12-13; problems and challenges, 16-17; Sherpas' role in, 13-14
mountains, 4-5

N
Native Americans, 20, 22
Nepal, 8, 9, 14

O
Owen, William, 23
oxygen, 16

P
Pacific Ocean, 36
plate tectonics: Chimborazo and, 36-37; Kilimanjaro and, 28; Mount Everest and, 10-11; Teton Range and, 22
plateau: Kilimanjaro, 28; Tibet, 8
puja ceremony, 15
Purtscheller, Ludwig, 26

R
Rebmann, Johannes, 26
rifting, 22

S
savanna, 26
sheep, 34-25
Sherpas, 12-15
Shira Cone, 30, 31
Shoshone people, 22
Stevenson, James, 23
stratovolcanoes, 28, 36

T
tectonic plates. *See* plate tectonics
Tenzing Norgay, 12-14, 16
Teton Range, 18-23; features of, 20-21; first climbing of, 23; formation of, 22; maps, 5, 21
Tibet, 8, 9
trash, 17

U
Uhuru Peak, 26, 28-29, 31

V
volcanic mountains, 28, 36
volcanoes, 10, 28, 35, 36

W
Waugh, A. S., 9
weathering, 4
Whymper, Edward, 34

40